by BETTY POLISAR REIGOT ■ illustrated by KATHY HENDRICKSON

with illustrations by JOHN SPIERS

SCHOLASTIC INC.

New York Toronto London Auckland Sydney

ISBN 0-590-52839-4

12 11 10 9 8 7 6 5 4 3 2 1 5 6 7 8 9/9 0/0

Printed in the U.S.A. 23

First Scholastic printing, October 1995

Book design by Laurie Williams

Bees *is for Beatrice*

Acknowledgments

For their generous help in offering information, suggestions, and assistance, my thanks to Dr. Jerome G. Rozen, Jr., of the American Museum of Natural History; Dr. Charles D. Michener, of the University of Kansas; Dr. O. Van Laere, of the State Entomology Research Station, Belgium; and Stephen B. Bambara, of North Carolina State University.

CONTENTS

What are bees?

Bees are hairy insects with wings.
Bees, wasps, and ants are all related. Wasps look something like bees, but wasps are meat eaters. Bees are flower eaters.

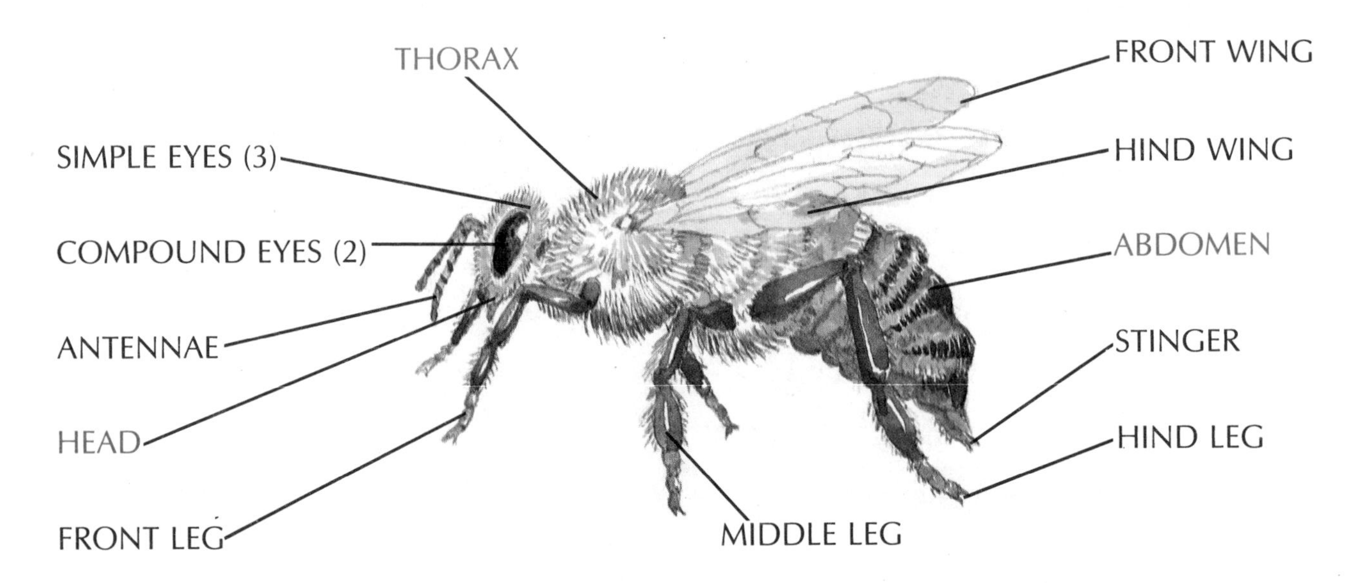

An insect's body has three parts—a head, a thorax, and an abdomen. An insect also has six legs.
Bees have two pairs of wings. When a bee is in a small space, such as its nest, the back pair of wings (hind wings) are tucked under the front wings next to the bee's body. When the bee flies, it spreads its wings and hooks the hind wings onto the front wings.

Do all bees look alike?

No. There are thousands and thousands of different kinds of bees.

Most of them are black, sometimes with yellow marks. Some are shiny blue, or green, or purple, or even red. Many have white hairs that make them look gray.

Some bees are thin. Some are chunky.

Some are as tiny as the "o" on this page. Some are giant bees about as long as your thumb. Most are an in-between size.

Do bees live with other bees?

Most bees live alone all their lives. A bee that lives alone is called a *solitary bee*.

Some bees begin their lives as solitary bees. Later they live with other bees—usually their own grown children.

Bees that live with other bees are called *social bees*. They belong to a *colony*. A colony may have just two, or three, or four, bees. Some colonies have many more.

There are some very social bees that belong to colonies with thousands of bees.

The place where bees live is called a *nest*.

One kind of solitary bee is called a carpenter bee. The scientific name for this carpenter bee is *Xylocopa virginica*.

One kind of social bee is the honeybee. Honeybees live together in a colony. The scientific name of this honeybee is *Apis mellifera*.

Where do you find bees?

Wherever flowers bloom there are usually bees. It may be a meadow, a garden, a city park, a windowsill, a farm, an orchard, a mountain, a jungle. On warm, sunny days, bees can be seen anywhere, if flowers are there.

What do bees eat?

There are two parts of a flower that bees need for food. One is *nectar*—the sweet juice of a flower. Bees suck nectar with a tubelike tongue that is part of their *proboscis* (pro-**bah-**sis).

The other flower food that bees eat is *pollen*. A bee usually takes the tiny yellow grains of pollen from flowers with the hairs on its front legs. Then it may put the pollen in its mouth.

Does each bee find its own food?

Each solitary bee finds its own food. A solitary bee that is going to be a mother brings food back to the nest for the babies she will have.

In a colony of honeybees, the older bees usually hunt for food. They bring it back for other bees in the nest. They also have a way to let the bees in the nest know where they may get the food themselves.

How does a bee bring food back to the nest?

A bee has two stomachs. One is like a storage bin. It is called a *crop*. Nectar is stored there. The crop can stretch a lot. A bee can carry a lot of nectar.

Some bees carry a little pollen in the crop, too. But bees usually carry pollen another way. Their hairy bodies get dusted all over with the powdery, yellow stuff. Most solitary bees brush the pollen onto their hind legs and abdomen. When they get back to the nest, they brush it off.

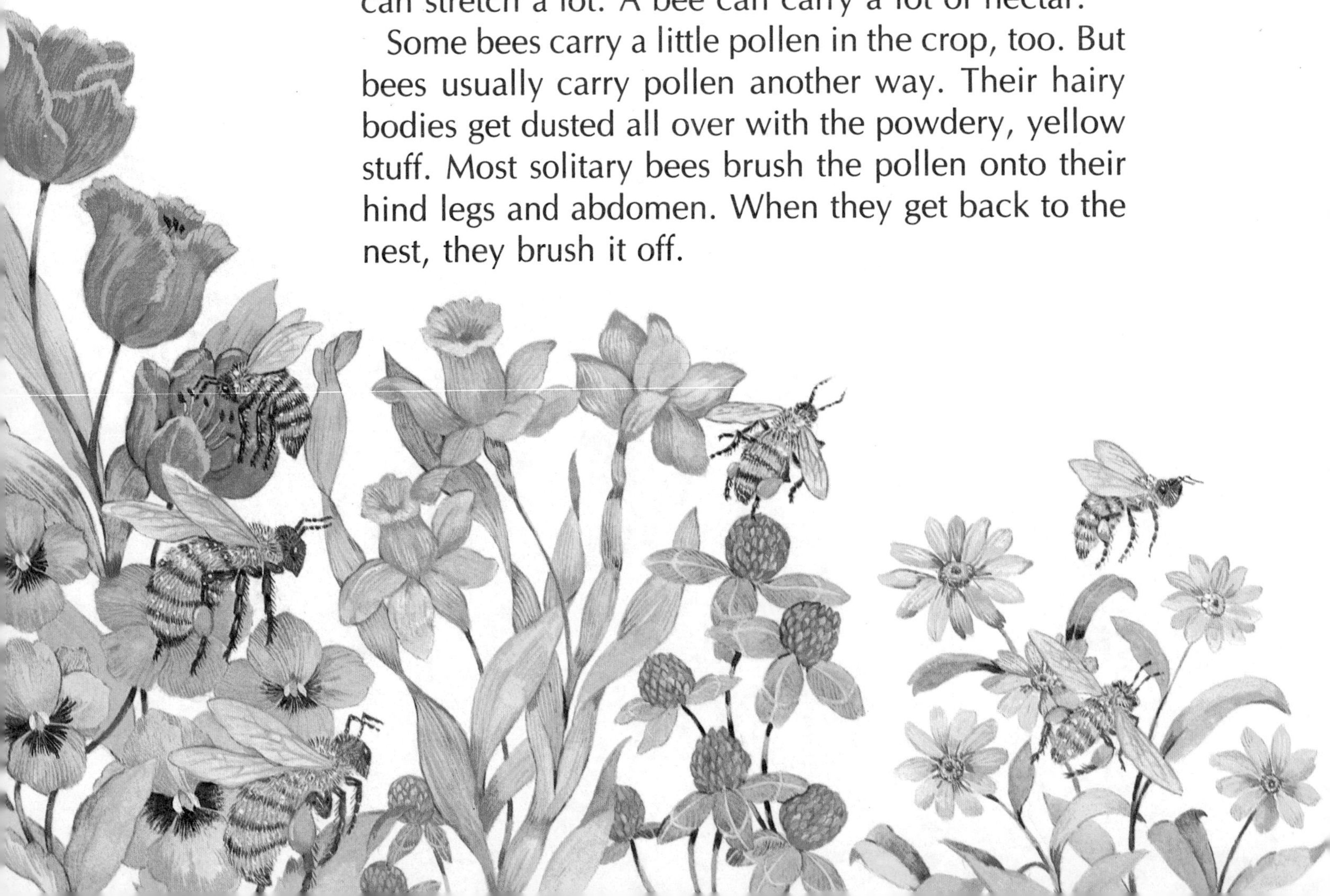

There are rows of stiff hairs on a bee's legs. A bee uses these stiff hairs like a brush and comb to get the pollen out of its body hairs.

When honeybees brush and comb pollen out of their body hairs, they mix in some nectar from their crop. This makes the pollen stick together. Their front and middle legs pass the pollen back to the hind legs.

The hind legs have "baskets." The basket is really a flat, wide part of each leg. One hind leg pushes the pollen into the basket on the other hind leg.

Sometimes you can see bees doing this as they stay in the air over a flower. Long hairs around the baskets keep the pollen from falling out.

When the baskets are full, a honeybee looks as if it's wearing short, baggy pants. Now it flies back to the nest.

How does a bee feed itself?

A bee stores food in its crop. It uses its other stomach for its own food. When a bee is hungry, it lets food out of its crop into its own private stomach.

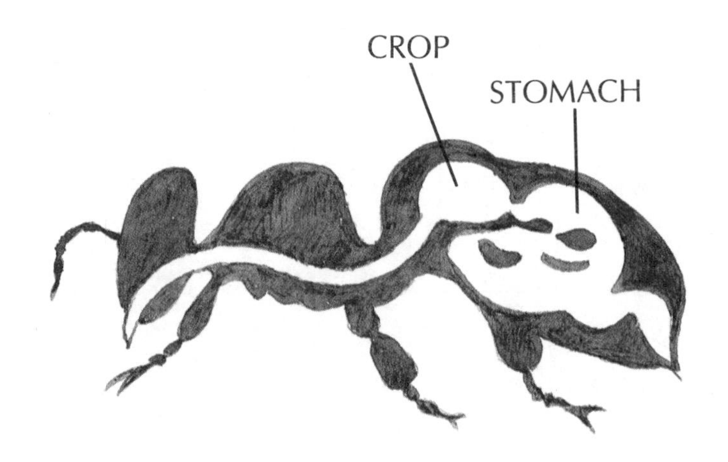

How does a bee feed other bees?

Solitary bees do not feed other adult bees.

But when honeybees come back to the nest with food, the other bees rush over to them. Food is passed out of the crop through the proboscis to the hungry bees in the nest. These bees eat some of the food and pass some along to other bees in the colony.

Some of the food gets stored in the nest. It is used to feed the young bees. It is kept for rainy days when bees don't fly and for winter when no flowers bloom.

The food bees eat and how they eat are very important to us. Why?

Bees fly from flower to flower to get food. If nectar is deep inside a flower, the bee with a long tongue can get it. The kinds of bees that have short tongues go to flowers where nectar is easier to reach.

There are orchid bees, sunflower bees, cactus bees, and other kinds of bees with flower names. These bees are named for the flower they usually go to for food.

Most bees go to the same kind of flower for a while. It may be just for a day or for a few days. Then a bee will change to another flower.

Flowers are the parts of a plant where seeds form.

A flower must get pollen from another flower of the same kind to form seeds. It is from a seed that a new plant grows.

Some flowers get pollen because the wind carries the pollen over from another flower.

Some flowers get pollen from other insects that come for food.

The creature that probably does the best job of bringing pollen from one flower to another is the bee.

A lot of pollen that falls on a bee's hairy body gets left on other flowers the bee visits. Now new seeds can form. New plants can grow.

If there were no bees, we would not have many beautiful flowers. We would not have many plants and trees. We would not have many fruits and vegetables that grow from seeds.

Bees don't care about our having beautiful flowers and food to eat. They just happen to spread pollen because they are looking for food for themselves.

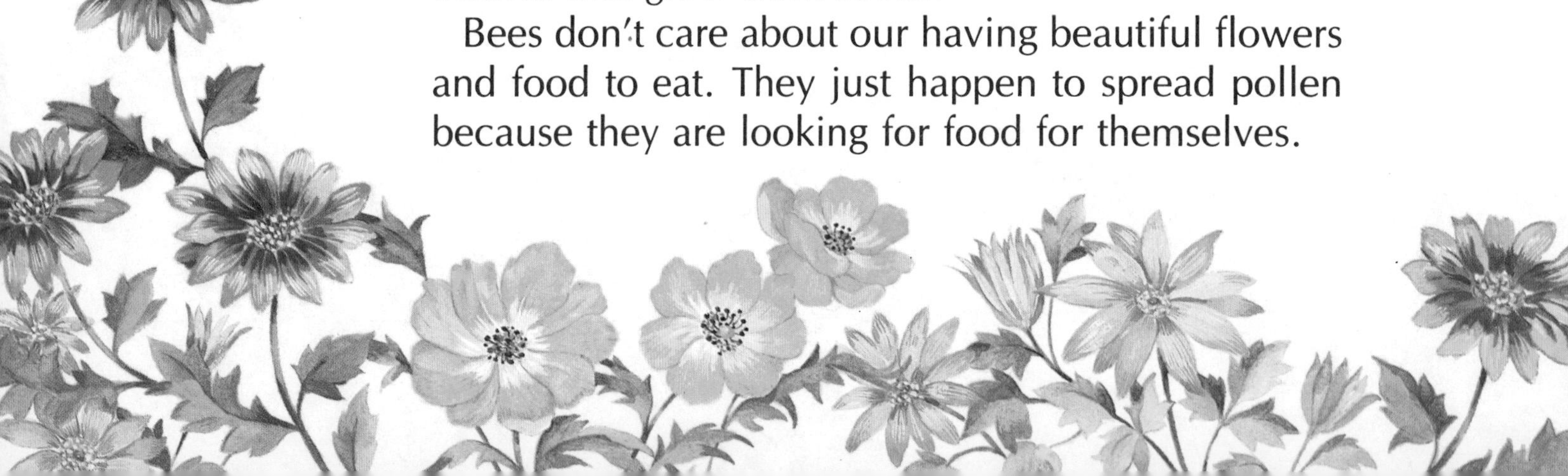

How do bees get to be bees?

Like other insects, bees change shape from the time they are born until they become adults.

A bee begins life as an egg. The egg turns into a *larva,* then a *pupa,* and then an adult bee.

How do the changes happen? How long do they take?

Most bee eggs hatch into *larvae* (**lar**-vee) a few days after the eggs are laid.

EGG

Larvae are white and fat. They look like worms—no legs and not much hair. A larva has a mouth at one end and eats lots of *bee bread*. Bee bread is a mixture of nectar and pollen.

LARVA

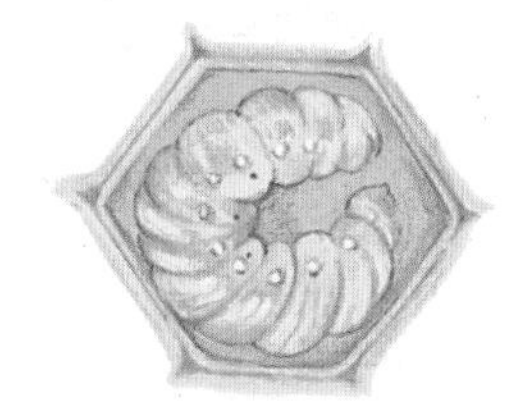

Some larvae turn into *pupae* (**pew**-pee) in two or three weeks. Others stay as larvae for several months. There are larvae that stay that way for a few years.

Some larvae spin silk *cocoons*. The cocoon is a wrapping for the pupa. A pupa doesn't eat and doesn't move. But it takes the shape of an adult bee. Usually in a few days, the young adult bee breaks out of the cocoon.

PUPA

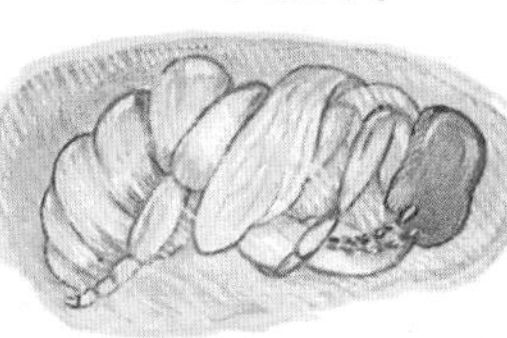

Now the bee begins its busy life.

Do bee eggs, larvae, and pupae need to be taken care of?

A solitary mother bee leaves a supply of nectar and pollen with the egg. She leaves enough for the larva to eat until it becomes a pupa. Pupae don't eat.

In a honeybee colony, some of the young adults are *nurse bees*. They keep feeding the larvae all the time until the larvae become pupae. Other *worker bees* in the colony keep the nest clean.

How long do bees live?

Most adult bees live only a few weeks.

A young adult that comes out of its cocoon in the fall may hibernate in the nest all winter. Once it becomes active it doesn't live very long.

How do bees get around? How do they know what to do?

Bees fly.

Bees see. A bee has two big eyes, one on each side of its head. It has three more eyes—small ones—on top of its head.

Bees see all the colors we see except red. They can see a color we cannot see—ultraviolet. The ultraviolet color of some flowers shows more clearly where the nectar and pollen are. This makes it easier for the bee to find its food.

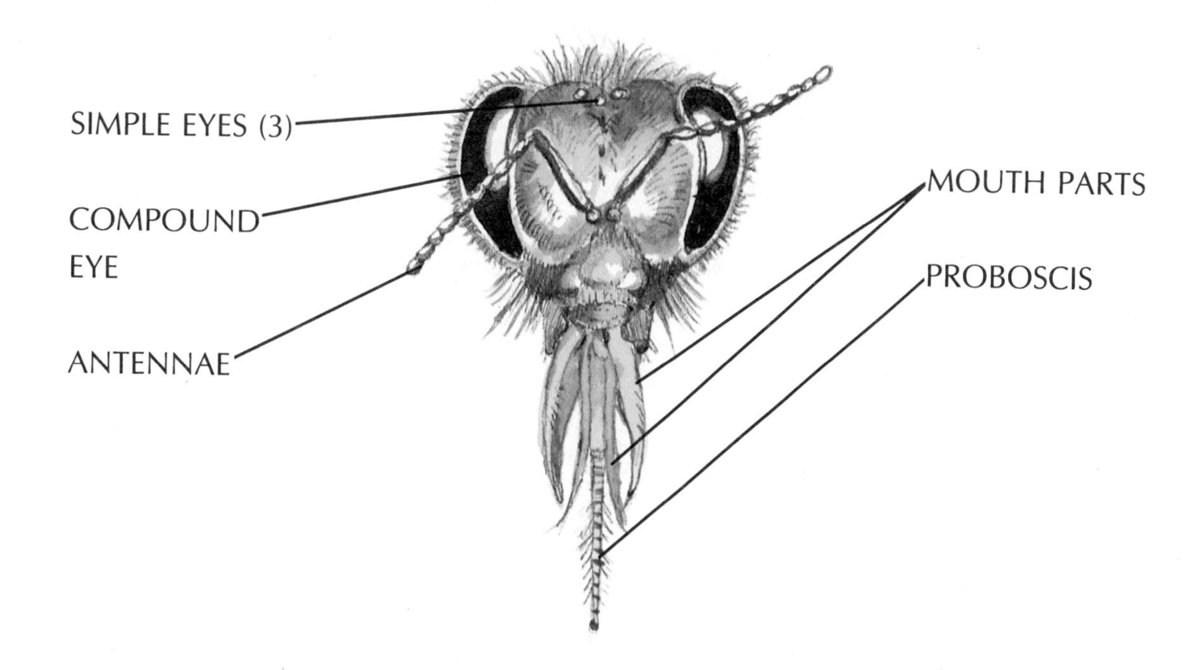

Bees use the position of the sun to guide them to food and to get back home. Ultraviolet rays of the sun come through clouds that are not too thick. So bees know where the sun is on a cloudy day.

Bees can tell the difference between shapes. This helps them find different flowers. It helps them pick out big objects, like the edge of a woods. Big objects keep bees from getting lost. They guide the bee back to its nest.

We usually see bees flitting about in sunshine. But bees spend most of their lives in dark nests. Bees get around in their nests by smelling, feeling, and touching. They do this mainly with their *antennae* (an-**ten**-ee).

Experiments with bees show they can be trained to come to a certain color, a certain odor, and a certain shape. They can learn these things. But scientists do not believe bees think the way humans can.

SOLITARY BEES

What are the nests of solitary bees like?

A solitary bee's nest is where a single adult female lives. It is also where her babies grow up. But not all the nests of solitary bees are alike.

Some solitary bees make nests in hollow trees and in stems and stalks of plants and weeds.

Other kinds of solitary bees make nests of leaves and pebbles and a sticky sap, called *resin*. The resin holds it all together. This kind of nest is out in the open.

The carpenter bee makes a tunnel in wood. The bee uses wood chips mixed with saliva to divide the tunnel into separate cells, one for each egg.

The mason bee builds a nest on a brick wall. It is made of clay and saliva.

Most solitary bees dig nests in the soil. Usually, the nest is a tunnel. How far down it goes depends on the kind of bee.

The tunnel may be only about 100 millimeters deep (a few inches) or as long as two meters (over two yards). The tunnel is a little wider than the body of the bee that digs it.

The mining bee digs
a tunnel in the ground.

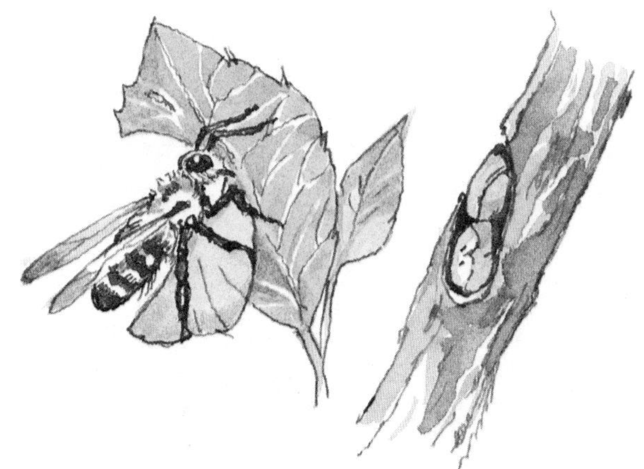

The leaf-cutter bee makes its
nest inside a small branch or twig.
It cuts oval pieces of leaf from
the living plant to line the cells.

Where do solitary bees keep their babies?

The mother bee builds *cells,* like tiny rooms, in the nest. Each cell is for one bee egg.

Some kinds of bees build about six cells. And some kinds of bees build as many as 40 cells.

The cells may be on the sides of the tunnel or at the end. Some cells are along branches of the tunnel.

What is the cell made of?

The cell of a solitary bee is made of earth, pieces of leaves, and pebbles stuck together with resin. It is lined with a thin coat of *beeswax* or of a material that is something like cellophane. The cell is usually very smooth.

What goes on in the nest? How do things get done?

The female solitary bee does all the work. After mating, she builds the nest, digs the tunnel, and makes as many cells as she will need.

She must find food for herself and bring some back to the nest. She places a ball of food in the cell—enough for the whole growing period of a larva. She lays an egg on top of the food. Then she closes the cell with soil, or resin, or leaf pieces. She does that for all the eggs she lays.

Some mother bees fly away as soon as they close the last cell. Then they may build another nest in some other place.

A few solitary mother bees may stay with their offspring for a little while. Other mother bees stay until their babies hatch into adults.

Where do solitary male bees live?

Solitary male bees live outside the nest. Some burrow in soil for the night. Some sleep in flowers. Some sleep together with other male bees in a curled leaf.

Males from different families of bees will often join one another. They can be a very large group. They sleep together night after night on the same stem. They hang on the stem with their strong jaws. These groups are called *sleeping clusters*.

Once in a while a female will belong to a sleeping cluster.

A solitary male bee snuggles in the petals of this flower.

Are solitary bees' nests far apart?

Many solitary bees build nests far from other bees' nests.

But some kinds of solitary bees build nests close to other solitary bees. There are places where hundreds, even thousands, of nests are right next to one another. Each one is the home of a single bee.

Sometimes a solitary bee will share a tunnel entrance with another bee or even a few bees.

HONEYBEES

Honeybees are different from most other bees. Why?

All bees make honey and spread pollen. But the common honeybee—*Apis mellifera*—is a very special bee. It is one of the very few kinds of bees that always lives in colonies.

People have learned how to take honey and beeswax from the colony and not bother the bees. Beekeepers have been doing this for about 4,000 years.

Some people become beekeepers as a hobby. Most beekeepers sell honey and beeswax for money. They rent beehives to farmers who need bees to help them raise fruits and vegetables. There are many books about how to keep bees.

Where are honeybee nests?

Many bee colonies are in man-made hives instead of nests. Most of these hives are wooden boxes that are made of sections, one on top of the other. The beekeeper lifts off a section to get the honey and beeswax. The bees stay in the hive.

Nests in the wild are usually in hollow trees. Some honeybees nest in a deep hole in the ground. Some make their nests in the side of a cliff or bank.

What does a honeybee's nest look like?

The nest of the common honeybee has many cells. Each cell—made of beeswax—has six sides. A shape with six sides is called a *hexagon*. Each side is part of another six-sided cell, or hexagon.

The hexagons all connect and make a layer that has a lovely design. The layer of cells is back-to-back with another layer of hexagon cells. This double layer of cells is called a *honeycomb*.

There may be ten or twelve honeycombs in one honeybee nest.

There are three different sizes of cells in the honeycomb.

The smallest cells are for bees that become workers. These are called *brood cells*. Other small cells, near the brood cells, are used for storing pollen. Farther away, usually above the brood cells, are still more small cells where the bees store honey.

Larger cells—usually built in the lower corners of the honeycomb—are for the eggs that grow into male bees, or *drones*.

There is one kind of cell in the nest that is not a hexagon. It is much bigger and sort of round. There are only five or six of these special cells in a large colony. Each of them contains a bee called a *gyne* (**jine**—rhymes with **line**). One gyne will be the next *queen* of the colony.

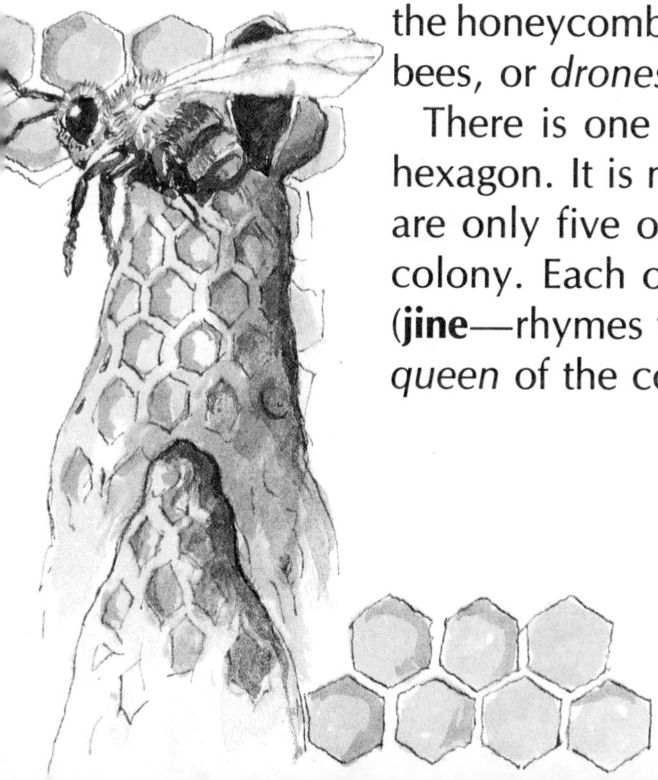

How are the worker, queen, and drone different from one another?

Workers and queens are female bees. Drones are males. Most of the colony is made up of workers. There is only one queen.

Workers, queens, and drones all do different jobs. A colony needs these three kinds of honeybees to survive.

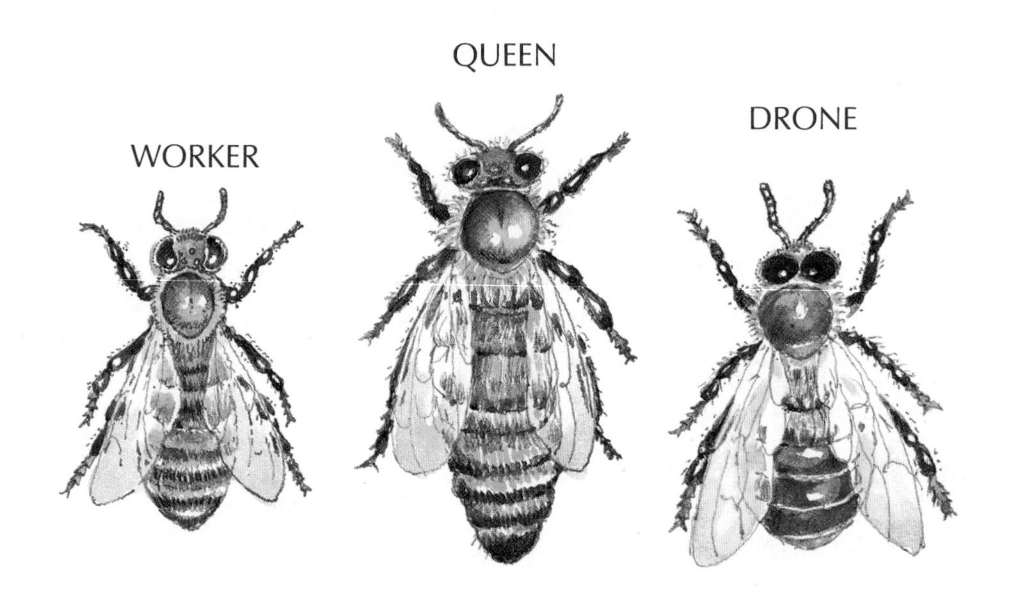

What do workers do?

The younger workers have special jobs to do:

Some build cells, repair them, and keep them clean.

Others feed the larvae in the brood cells. They close the cell with a cap of beeswax just before a larva turns into a pupa.

Some fill the storage cells with honey or pollen brought in by field bees.

Some keep the brood cells at the right temperature. If it is too cold, they huddle together to make a living blanket. If it gets too hot, they send messages to other bees in the colony to bring water. They spread drops of water over the brood cells. Then they fan the air with their wings to cool the nest.

Some feed and look after the queen. They lick her and keep her clean.

Older workers usually do other jobs:

Some guard the nest against wasps, mice, or other enemies. Bees sting an enemy to drive it off or kill it. A worker bee's stinger stays inside its victim. And without its stinger, the bee dies.

If a field mouse—or any other creature—comes too close to their nest, guard bees usually fly out and attack it.

Some old workers are field bees that go out and find food. They bring it back to the nest. They also "tell" the other bees where to go for the food. How they do this is one of the amazing things that happens in nature. (You will read about this on page 40.)

Some worker bees find new nest sites for the colony.

Some just crawl around the nest. They feel and smell with their antennae. They find out what needs to be done. They do it. And they are there to defend the nest in case it is attacked.

What does the queen do?

The queen lays eggs—lots of eggs. She is like an egg machine.

Some colonies have about 100,000 bees. That many people living in one place would be a big city.

It is easy to tell the queen from the other bees. She is the largest bee and has a circle of workers around her all the time. They all face her.

What do the drones do?

Most of the time drones stay out of the way. Some of them go to other colonies. Workers in the colony feed them for a while.

The drones have just one job. It is to mate with a gyne.

What happens at mating time?

There can be only one queen in a colony. When an adult gyne breaks out of her cell, she makes sure no other gynes are in the nest. If there are, they fight until only one is left. Sometimes the workers kill the extra gynes.

Then, on some lovely warm afternoon, the gyne leaves the nest. She flies high in the sky. Drones fly after her and several may mate with her.

The drones who have mated with the gyne drop to the ground and die. The gyne enters the nest. Now she is the queen bee. She spends the rest of her life laying eggs. Queen bees often live four or five years—a lot longer than most bees.

What happens to the other drones?

The other drones return to the colony. But they are not allowed to stay very long. The workers are now busy taking care of the queen and the babies and the nest.

After a while, the workers push or pull the drones out of the nest. They don't let them in again. Most of the drones starve. Some of them may find a home in another colony.

How do honeybees care for their babies?

One honeybee egg is placed in each cell. When the egg turns into a larva, it begins to fill up the cell. The cell is left open.

Young adult bees, or nurse bees, put food in the cell with their proboscis. They do this many times a day.

For the first couple of days all the larvae get *bee milk*—a white liquid that comes from special glands in the nurse bee's head. It is usually mixed with nectar or honey from the bee's crop.

After two days, the larvae that will grow into workers or drones are given bee bread—a mixture of bee milk, nectar or honey, and pollen.

Gyne larvae are fed only bee milk. (It is sometimes called royal jelly.) Gynes never get bee bread.

About a week later, the nurse bees close the cells with caps of beeswax. The larvae spin their cocoons. They turn into pupae. The cells stay closed until the adult bees come out.

1. The queen bee lays an egg in each cell.
2. The egg becomes a larva. As it grows, the larva is fed by a nurse bee. The larva grows until it fills the cell.
3. The larva does not need to be fed anymore. The nurse bee caps the cell with beeswax, and the larva spins its cocoon.
4. The larva turns into a pupa.
5. A honeybee is born!

How do bees make honey?

When bees drink nectar from flowers, part of it gets turned into another kind of sugary liquid. They bring that out of their crop and let some of the liquid evaporate. The sugary juice gets thicker. Now it is honey.

Honeybees store this honey in cells. They put a cap of beeswax on the cell. This keeps the honey from drying up and getting hard.

How do honeybees let other bees know where food is?

An Austrian scientist, Karl von Frisch, did many experiments to find out how honeybees give messages to one another.

He put a dish of sweet syrup outside. One day a bee found and tasted the syrup. Soon lots of bees came from the same hive to get syrup. How did they know where to come?

Looking through a pane of glass, von Frisch watched the bees in their hive. He saw that when a bee finds a new source of food, she comes back to the nest and does a little dance.

These patterns show the different dances that bees do.

ROUND DANCE

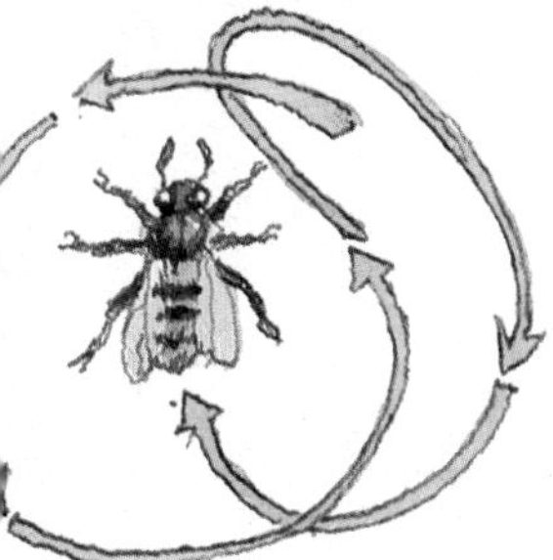

Food is nearby.

FIGURE EIGHT DANCE

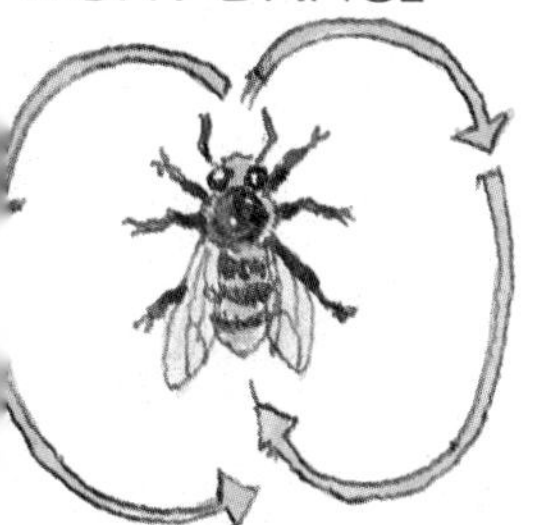

Food is not too near but not too far.

If the food is nearby, the bee does a round dance. If the food is not near, the bee dances a figure eight. If the food is far away, the bee waggles its abdomen when it gets to the middle of the figure eight.

The hive is dark, and the other bees cannot see the dance. But they crowd around the dancer and follow her. They touch her with their antennae. They feel the vibrations of her movements. She gives them each some food. They smell it and taste it.

Many scientists believe that the kind of dance, how fast it is, the number of turns and waggles, and the way the bee points her body are all messages about just where there is food. Now the bees know what kind of food to look for and where to get it.

TAIL-WAGGING DANCE

Food is far away.

This shows the way a honeybee does a "tail-wagging" dance on the surface of the honeycomb. The arrows show the direction the bee takes in the dance. The other bees follow. The honeybee wags its tail where you see the broken lines.

Other scientists believe the dances do not give all the information bees need to find food. The bee may dance to excite the other bees and let them know, "I visited this flower and brought back some of its nectar and pollen. Here is a taste. Smell it on my body. Now go and find the flower."

The bees use their great sense of smell to search for the odor of this flower. Each of the bees now ready to look for food flies out and upward, making circles. She can feel where the wind is blowing from and picks out the odors it carries.

Then the bee may start downward, making wider circles until she catches the right odor. When she does, she flies zigzag into the wind, sometimes losing and then regaining the scent. She follows the right scent until she finds the right flower food source. It will be the same as what she tasted and smelled in the hive.

Do honeybees have other ways of giving messages?

Yes. There are chemicals, called *pheromones* (**fer**-a-moans), that come from a bee's body. Other bees smell or touch the pheromones and get the messages.

One kind of message is an alarm. Guard bees at the next entrance may see robber bees, or a wasp, or some other creature trying to get in. The guards' bodies produce an alarm pheromone. The other bees smell this and come out to attack and sting the enemy.

Bees also leave messages about where there is food, or water, or a new nest. They leave an odor that the other bees can follow. The odor is like a sign that says, "This way to food," or "This way to water," or "This way to the new nest."

One pheromone comes only from the queen. It is called *queen substance*. It keeps workers from building more queen cells.

Bees around the queen take queen substance with their mouth parts and their antennae. They pass it along to other workers in the colony. These workers pass it on to still others, until all the bees in the colony have some.

Some scientists believe that queen substance makes each bee feel it belongs to its colony. So bees stay together in the same colony—their colony. That way the colony continues.

If the queen dies, there is no queen substance. If a queen is not replaced, the colony dies out. Usually, if there is no queen substance, the workers begin at once to build gyne cells for a new queen.

What happens when a honeybee nest gets too crowded?

Honeybee colonies grow quite large. They then divide.

When it is time to divide, one of the bees breaks into a run and makes a buzzing noise with its wings. As it runs, it touches other bees. They start a buzzing run. Soon many bees are running and buzzing.

Suddenly, about half the bees in the colony buzz right out of the nest. The old queen flies along with them. This is called *swarming*. The swarm will form a new colony.

The bees that stay in the old colony have a new gyne that becomes their queen.

The swarm of bees flies to a nearby branch and waits there.

Meanwhile, the bees that danced in the nest to give messages about food are out nest-hunting. Now they return to the swarm. This time their dances will tell where there is a place to build a new nest.

One bee will dance longest. Her dance will be more lively than the others'. She is saying that she has found the best place. Other bees will fly to the place and look it over. Then they will lead the swarm to the new site.

It may take a while before the bees settle in a new nest. Before they left the old colony, the swarming bees filled their crops with honey to have food if they get hungry.

As soon as the bees reach the new site, they make honeycombs and store their food. The queen lays eggs. The workers take care of the cells and the young. A new colony is formed.

What and where are "killer bees"?

A while ago, some honeybees were brought from Africa to Brazil, in South America, for experiments. By accident, some of the bees escaped.

In Africa, where it is warm, flowers bloom all year. African bees are used to getting food whenever they need it. They don't have to store it. Instead, they reproduce many more bees and swarm often to find new nests. Otherwise their nests would get too crowded.

If anyone or anything disturbs their nest, a few thousand bees will fly out quickly to attack. They are smaller than the bees in our parts of the world, and their sting is not any worse. But they will follow the intruder for almost a mile. They also take longer to calm down. That is why they have been nicknamed "killer bees." Scientists prefer to call them Africanized bees.

Africanized bees have been heading northward from Brazil. They travel about 300 miles each year. They are now in southern and southwestern parts of the United States. As they approach the north, they may mate more with European bees to survive the cold climate.